Novels for Students, Volume 13

Staff

Editor: Elizabeth Thomason.

Contributing Editors: Anne Marie Hacht, Michael L. LaBlanc, Ira Mark Milne, Jennifer Smith, Carol Ullmann.

Managing Editor, Content: Dwayne D. Hayes.

Managing Editor, Product: David Galens.

Publisher, Literature Product: Mark Scott.

Literature Content Capture: Joyce Nakamura, *Managing Editor*. Sara Constantakis, *Editor*.

Research: Victoria B. Cariappa, *Research Manager*. Sarah Genik, Ron Morelli, Tamara Nott, Tracie A. Richardson, *Research Associates*. Nicodemus Ford, *Research Assistant*.

Permissions: Maria Franklin, *Permissions Manager*. Kim Davis, *Permissions Associate*.

Manufacturing: Mary Beth Trimper, *Manager, Composition and Electronic Prepress*. Evi Seoud, *Assistant Manager, Composition Purchasing and Electronic Prepress*. Stacy Melson, *Buyer*.

Imaging and Multimedia Content Team: Barbara Yarrow, *Manager*. Randy Bassett, *Imaging Supervisor*. Robert Duncan, Dan Newell, Luke Rademacher, *Imaging Specialists*. Pamela A. Reed, *Imaging Coordinator*. Leitha Etheridge-Sims, Mary Grimes, David G. Oblender, *Image Catalogers*. Robyn V. Young, *Project Manager*. Dean Dauphinais, *Senior Image Editor*. Kelly A. Quin, *Image Editor*.

Product Design Team: Pamela A. E. Galbreath, *Senior Art Director*. Michael Logusz, *Graphic Artist*.

Copyright Notice

of the publisher and verified to the satisfaction of the publisher will be corrected in future editions.

This publication is a creative work fully protected by all applicable copyright laws, as well as by misappropriation, trade secret, unfair competition, and other applicable laws. The authors and editors of this work have added value to the underlying factual material herein through one or more of the following: unique and original selection, coordination, expression, arrangement, and classification of the information. All rights to this publication will be vigorously defended.

Brideshead Revisited

Evelyn Waugh 1945

Introduction

Evelyn Waugh's novels written before 1945 are typically satiric and filled with dry humor and sarcasm, and many critics view *Brideshead Revisited* as heralding a change in Waugh's writing style. *Brideshead Revisited* presents a more nostalgic story based on the main character's memories of a wealthy English Catholic family he befriended before World War II. In an England where most people are Protestant, being Catholic makes the family—despite their land ownership and high social status—a minority, subject to a degree of prejudice. Many of the characters and events in the novel reflect Waugh's life when he was in school and later as an adult.

Brideshead Revisited was the first of Waugh's novels to come to the attention of the American public. In fact, soon after the publication of Brideshead Revisited, Life magazine printed an interview with Waugh. But critics were split over the quality of the novel, and some have criticized it for being too romantic and lacking the brilliance of Waugh's other novels. James Carens in The Satiric Art of Evelyn Waugh notes that even though the critic and author Edmund Wilson was an admirer of Waugh's earlier works, he condemned Brideshead Revisited as a "disastrous" novel. In contrast, Carens notes that the review in Catholic World magazine praised the novel, calling it "a work of art."

Author Biography

The religious issues appearing in *Brideshead Revisited* concerned Evelyn Waugh from a relatively young age. Born Evelyn Arthur St. John Waugh on October 28, 1903, in the comfortable London suburb of Hampstead, England, Evelyn was the youngest son of Arthur Waugh, a devout member of the Anglican Church. He was educated at Lancing, a preparatory school that specialized in educating the sons of Anglican clergy. Like all students at Lancing, Evelyn was required to attend chapel every morning and evening and three times on Sundays. According to Waugh in his unfinished autobiography, *A Little Learning: The Early Years*, he does not remember thinking that these requirements were unreasonable.

Arthur Waugh worked as a publisher, critic, author, and editor, which provided Evelyn with daily exposure to books and writing. In addition, Evelyn's father, together with his mother, Catherine Charlotte Raban Waugh, regularly read aloud to both their sons. At age seven, Evelyn had already written a short story, and by age nine, with a group of friends, he had produced a magazine. Eventually, his older brother, Alec, went on to write best-selling novels and travel books.

Waugh's years as an adult were remarkably similar to the experiences of Charles Ryder, the protagonist in *Brideshead Revisited*. By the time

Waugh left Lancing for Oxford, he reported that he was no longer a Christian, thanks in part to an instructor who encouraged him to think skeptically about religion, as well as to his extensive reading of philosophers of the Enlightenment (a movement in the eighteenth century that advocated the use of reason in the reappraisal of accepted ideas and social institutions). While at Oxford, Waugh studied some and drank and socialized a great deal with an artistic and literary crowd. He left Oxford before receiving a degree to attend art school.

The next few years saw Waugh drinking too much. He was unhappy and unsure as to his life's calling. He left art school to become a teacher but was fired from three schools in less than two years. Finally, in 1927, he began to write on a regular basis and a year later published his first novel, *Decline and Fall*. The book, a humorous and satiric look at a young man's efforts to find his way in a world where evil is rewarded and good is punished, was a controversial success. That same year he married, but the marriage soon broke up because of his wife's infidelity.

In 1930, Waugh became a Roman Catholic, his conversion brought about by his wife's unfaithfulness and by his disenchantment with modern society. In 1936, he received an annulment of his marriage and the next year married Laura Herbert, a member of a prominent Catholic family. They had six children. Just as his character Ryder does, Waugh traveled extensively to exotic places during the 1930s and 1940s, including Africa and

Central America. His travels provided fuel for many of his books.

By the time Europe was preparing for the second world war, Waugh was a well-respected author. But his patriotism, along with a sense that his life had become too comfortable, prompted him to pull some strings to receive a post with the Royal Marines in 1939—not an easy accomplishment at the age of thirty-six. According to Paul S. Burdett, Jr., in *World War II*, Waugh's health was suspect, his eyesight was limited, and "his physique tended toward the pudgy," but he showed himself to be an eager soldier. His wartime experiences informed his later novels, including *Brideshead Revisited*.

When he died in Somerset, England, in 1966, Waugh had published more than thirty books, fourteen of which were novels. He also published travel books, biographies, short stories, and essays, securing his position as one of the most respected English authors of the twentieth century. His reputation as a man with a bitingly sharp wit gave many people the impression that he was an uncaring person; but those who knew him tell of a man who was exceedingly generous with his money and time, especially to those in financial need and to aspiring writers.

Prologue

In *Brideshead Revisited*, Charles Ryder is a middle-aged captain in the British Army during World War II, stationed in the Scottish countryside in 1942. He organizes his troops to move them to another location via train overnight. When the sun comes up, he realizes that the new encampment is in England near a mansion whose owners he once knew.

Book One

Chapters One-Four

In 1923, Charles is at Oxford studying history, and in his third term he meets fellow student Sebastian Flyte, the son of a wealthy Catholic family, who carries around a stuffed bear named Al. Sebastian asks Charles to lunch with his friends (including Anthony Blanche), who are witty and worldly. Sebastian later takes Charles on a day trip to the countryside, where they have a picnic. On this excursion, Sebastian brings Charles to his family's home, a mansion named Brideshead. Charles is very impressed with Sebastian.

The following year, after Charles has been

associating with Sebastian and his friends for a while, Charles' cousin Jasper scolds him for hanging around with a bad set of people. Charles is not swayed. Anthony Blanche invites Charles to dinner, where Anthony discusses in great detail the members of Sebastian's family and their peculiarities.

Charles travels to London to spend the summer vacation with his father. Their time together is uncomfortable, and Charles refers to it as a "war." Sebastian sends Charles a telegram stating that he is gravely injured, and that Charles must come to his aid at once. When Charles arrives at Brideshead, he discovers that Sebastian has merely cracked a small bone in his foot. Charles meets Julia, Sebastian's sister.

Charles spends the rest of summer break with Sebastian, and he later recalls having a wonderful time, "very near heaven during those languid days." They stay at the Brideshead mansion, where Charles begins to paint a mural in one of the rooms. He meets Cordelia, Sebastian's youngest sister, and his brother, Brideshead. The issue of the family's Catholicism comes up in conversations a number of times. The two friends also travel to Venice, Italy, to visit Sebastian's father, Lord Marchmain, and his mistress, Cara.

Chapters Five-Eight

Charles and Sebastian return to Oxford in the fall, where they discover that Anthony Blanche has failed his classes and has moved to Munich. The two friends begin to feel older and less like pursuing their frivolous lifestyle of the previous year, and Sebastian puts away his stuffed bear. Charles begins to take art classes. Rex Mottram, Julia's boyfriend, invites them to a party in London, and they end up at a whorehouse. Later that evening, the police stop Sebastian while he is driving drunk, and everyone, including Charles, is sent to the jail. Rex bails them out. Charles goes to Brideshead mansion for the Christmas holidays, and Lady Marchmain talks to him about becoming a Catholic. Sebastian is drinking even more heavily and is worried that Charles is watching his behavior at his mother's request.

There is an ugly scene at Brideshead mansion during the Easter break in which Sebastian is drunk and then leaves. There is another drunken scene at school later. Sebastian fails his classes at Oxford, and Lady Marchmain warns him that she will send him to live with an old priest if he does not straighten up. Sebastian goes to Venice to be with his father, instead, and Lady Marchmain plans to have Mr. Samgrass, a history don (tutor), watch over him and take him on a vacation to the Middle East when he returns from Italy. Charles tells his father that he wants to leave Oxford to attend art school.

Charles does, in fact, go to Paris to attend art school. Sebastian and Mr. Samgrass return from their trip. Charles comes to Brideshead mansion for Christmas and sees that Sebastian is drinking even more and looks ill. Everyone discovers that Sebastian left Mr. Samgrass during the trip and wandered about on his own for a time. Sebastian was found only after he couldn't pay his hotel bill, and the hotel management called his family. The whole family is on edge about Sebastian's depression and drinking, but he agrees to go on a hunt, which en-courages Lady Marchmain. They make sure he has no money so he cannot stop and get a drink at a pub, but Charles gives him money in secret. Sebastian is found later that day, at a pub, drunk. Lady Marchmain finds out and is very angry with Charles. Rex attempts to take Sebastian to a doctor he knows in Zurich who can help him with his alcoholism, but Sebastian gives him the slip and disappears. Rex visits Charles, looking for Sebastian. Charles and Rex go out to dinner, where Rex tells Charles of Lady Marchmain's illness and the Flyte family's money troubles. Rex and Julia get married in a small ceremony. Sebastian is not present.

Charles recalls the story of Rex and Julia: when Julia was a debutante, how she and Rex met, their courtship, and the problems with their engagement and marriage ceremony. Lady Marchmain believes that Rex is beneath Julia and demands that their engagement remain a secret although their news gets out. Rex wants a very fancy wedding, with important guests and at an important cathedral, but because he is not Catholic, this is not possible. He takes classes with a priest to become a Catholic, but he is not terribly bright. The Catholic wedding is eventually called off because

Julia's brother, Brideshead, discovers that Rex has been divorced. The wedding finally takes place at a Protestant church known for marrying couples in Rex and Julia's situation.

The spring of 1926 sees Charles leaving Paris for London because he feels he must be in his country of birth during its difficult economic times. The General Strike occurs, and Charles signs up to help distribute food. One evening he goes to a jazz bar and runs into Anthony Blanche, who reports having allowed Sebastian to stay with him in Marseilles. He says that Sebastian was still drinking heavily and was stealing things from him to sell and pawn. Julia asks Charles to come to see Lady Marchmain at the family's London house, as she is dying. Charles does so, then goes to Morocco to find Sebastian, as Lady Marchmain has asked to see him one last time before she dies. He finds Sebastian in a hospital in Fez, very ill from his drinking. He is with a German named Kurt, who is also ill. Sebastian cannot travel to England because of his poor health, so Charles stays for a week and helps him settle his financial affairs. Charles returns to England and agrees to paint four oils of the soon-to-be torn down Marchmain house in London, as requested by Brideshead. Lady Marchmain dies. Cordelia later tells Charles that Lady Marchmain's funeral mass was the last event at the family chapel at Brideshead before it was closed up.

Book Two

Chapters One-Five

The story now moves to the late 1930s, when Charles is a painter of some repute, primarily of buildings about to be razed. He is married to Celia, the sister of a fellow Oxford student, and they have two young children. He is returning from a two-year trip to Mexico and Central America, where he was drawing ruins. He meets Celia in New York City, and they leave for London on a ship. They seem to have a cool relationship although Celia is a very friendly woman who loves to entertain. They give a cocktail party on board the ship the first night and also discover that Julia is on board. A storm hits the ship, and Celia retires, seasick, to her room throughout the storm's duration, about three days. Charles and Julia get reacquainted during this time, and they eventually make love in Julia's stateroom. Charles recalls that Celia once had an affair, and Julia tells Charles of her failed marriage with Rex and of her stillborn daughter. Charles sends Celia to their home while he stays in London to set up his next art show and to see Julia.

Charles and Julia continue their affair in London, and his art show is a success. There is talk of war at the show. Anthony Blanche appears at the show's opening, and he and Charles go to a bar to talk about old times. He knows about Julia and Charles's affair, having heard people speak of it at a luncheon that day.

Charles and Julia have been together for two years but haven't sought divorces from their spouses. They are now at Brideshead, as is Rex. One evening, Brideshead arrives from London with the sudden news that he is getting married to Beryl Muspratt, a widow with three children. He also mentions that his fiancée probably will not come to Brideshead to see Charles and Julia, as she is a very proper Catholic woman and would disapprove of their living arrangements. He also expects that Julia and Rex and Charles will leave the mansion to make room for his new family. This greatly upsets Julia, and she begins to question whether she is a sinner in the eyes of her God. Rex arrives with his political friends and there is more talk of war.

Both Charles and Julia begin the process of divorcing their spouses. Rex gives patriotic speeches in the House of Commons, and the country is full of the talk of avoiding war with the Germans. Cordelia shows up at Brideshead after years as a nurse and aid worker in Spain. She has seen Sebastian; he is living in Tunis, still drinking heavily and ill but living at a monastery.

Brideshead marries Beryl. Given the increasing political tensions in Europe, Lord Marchmain decides to return to England and the Brideshead mansion with his mistress in the winter. He arrives seriously ill. Julia and Charles, who had moved out of Brideshead, move back to the mansion to be with Lord Marchmain. He tells Julia and Charles that he dislikes Brideshead's new wife, Beryl, and cannot imagine her as the lady of the manor after he dies.

He says he is seriously considering leaving the estate to Julia and Charles, which stuns them.

By Easter, Lord Marchmain is getting sicker and closer to death, and Brideshead demands that a priest be sent for. The priest comes, but Lord Marchmain sends him away because he is a nonpracticing Catholic. Charles is very disdainful of Brideshead's bringing in the priest. In June, Charles and Celia's divorce is final, and she marries again. In July, Lord Marchmain is unconscious, and Julia brings back the priest. Charles disagrees with this but is not surprised at her actions—he has seen her becoming more religious during the summer. The priest arrives, gives Lord Marchmain the final blessing, and he responds when the priest asks him if he is sorry for his sins. This apparent sign that Lord Marchmain has accepted Catholicism again overwhelms Charles, who kneels and says a short prayer. Julia decides that she can no longer be with Charles, in what she now sees as a sinful relationship.

Epilogue

The story ends where it began, with Charles as a captain in the British Army, encamped near the Brideshead mansion during World War II. Julia, who is overseas with Cordelia helping with the war effort, now owns the mansion. Brideshead is serving with the British cavalry in Palestine. Charles wanders around the old place, reminiscing, and bumps into a few of the staff still there. The family chapel is open, with a light burning upon the altar. Charles says a short prayer and leaves.

Characters

Mrs. Abel

Mrs. Abel is Edward Ryder's cook. According to Charles, her cooking skills are not very good.

Alfred

Alfred is one of Charles's cousins. Alfred gave advice to Charles's father about how to dress at school, which he steadfastly followed.

Aloysius

Aloysius is the teddy bear that Sebastian carries with him nearly everywhere he goes during his first year at Oxford, contributing to Sebastian's colorful reputation. Sebastian even goes so far as to refer to Aloysius as if he were a living creature, with likes and dislikes and moods. As Sebastian's drinking gets worse, he leaves Aloysius in a dresser drawer.

Antoine

See Anthony Blanche

Monsignor Bell

Lady Marchmain asks Monsignor Bell to give Sebastian a number of firm lectures about his failures at school and his heavy drinking. Sebastian's family later threatens to make him live with the monsignor if he does not straighten up, but Sebastian escapes this fate.

Anthony Blanche

Anthony is a student at Oxford and Sebastian's friend. He is a boisterous character, interested in food, wine, and having a good time. Charles refers to him as an "aesthete par excellence." There are indications that he is homosexual.

Everyone at school is in awe of Anthony. Charles remarks that even though he was barely older, Anthony seemed more mature and knowledgeable about the world than any of his other friends and acquaintances at Oxford. His background and experiences are somewhat romantic and mysterious. His mother lives in Argentina with his Italian stepfather, and Anthony has spent time with them traveling to exotic places. Anthony is always dropping names of famous people and places in his conversations with Sebastian and Charles.

Lady Brideshead

See Beryl Muspratt

Bridey

See Lord Brideshead Flyte

Cara

Cara is Lord Marchmain's mistress. She is a middle-aged, "well-preserved" woman, who speaks very plainly and honestly about her lover and his family.

Caroline

Caroline is Celia and Charles' infant daughter. She is born while Charles is overseas, and he takes very little interest in seeing her when he returns.

Collins

Collins is one of Charles's earliest friends at Oxford. Charles and Sebastian refer to him a number of times as someone who is studious and a solid person.

Earl of Brideshead

See Lord Brideshead Flyte

Effie

Effie is a prostitute at Ma Mayfield's, a whorehouse. She is with Sebastian, Charles, and Boy Mulcaster when they are stopped by the police for drunken driving.

There is also an "Effie" who works for Nanny when Brideshead is nearly empty and part of an army camp during World War II in the novel's epilogue.

Lord Brideshead Flyte

Brideshead is Sebastian's brother and the eldest son of Lord and Lady Marchmain. He gives the impression of someone who is more mature than his years, even though he is only three years older than Sebastian and Charles. He is very serious and does not have many friends. He is a devout Catholic.

Brideshead is unmarried throughout most of the novel and is searching for a vocation, having thought briefly about becoming a Jesuit priest or a politician. When Charles visits the family about ten years after the novel opens, Brideshead has become a prominent collector of matchbooks and spends most of his time on that hobby.

One day he suddenly announces that he has found a bride, Beryl Muspratt. She is the widow of another prominent matchbook collector and a devout Catholic with children.

Lady Cordelia Flyte

Cordelia is Sebastian's sister, Lord and Lady Marchmain's youngest daughter. When the book opens she is a precocious pre-teen and a serious Catholic. Catholicism is a common topic of her conversation.

Later in the novel, just before the outbreak of World War II, Cordelia works as a nurse in Spain, taking care of soldiers fighting in the Spanish Civil War. When Charles finds himself at Brideshead during World War II, she is reported to be in Palestine with Julia, working in some medical capacity. She never marries.

Lady Julia Flyte

Lady Julia is Sebastian's younger sister by a couple of years and the eldest daughter of Lord and Lady Marchmain. At the beginning of the novel, she is eighteen years old and involved in her debut to English society at parties in London. She is a classic beauty and is charming like her brother Sebastian, and her name appears in the newspapers frequently. She is a non-practicing Catholic, like Sebastian.

She eventually marries Rex Mottram, an aspiring politician, but the marriage is not a solid one. She tries to provide Rex with a child, but the daughter is stillborn. Julia runs into Charles and Celia on a cruise ship crossing the Atlantic from New York, where she has been pursuing a love affair. She and Charles fall in love by the time the ship docks in London. She and Charles seek separations and divorces from their respective spouses, but never marry each other.

Media Adaptations

- *Brideshead Revisited* was adapted as a television mini-series in 1982, starring Anthony Andrews, Jeremy Irons, Diana Quick, and Laurence Olivier, and produced by Granada Television. A six-volume VHS tape set of the series is available from Anchor Bay Entertainment.

- Harper Audio has produced a cassette recording of *Brideshead Revisited*, and Chivers Audio Books has produced a compact disc recording of the unabridged novel. Jeremy Irons narrates both versions, which were released in 2000.

- In 1994, Roger Parsley adapted the novel into a play entitled *Brideshead Revisited: A Play*.

Julia, through the death of her father, acquires a stronger sense of her Catholicism. When Charles returns to Brideshead during World War II, he discovers that she is with Cordelia in Palestine, working for the war effort. She never remarries.

Lord Sebastian Flyte

Sebastian is the charming youngest son of Lord and Lady Marchmain and Charles's closest friend at Oxford. They meet when Sebastian is drunk and vomits through Charles's window one night. The next day, Sebastian apologizes and asks Charles to lunch; they and others talk and drink until late in the afternoon.

Sebastian is not only charming; he is, in Charles's words, "magically beautiful." Charles becomes quite taken with Sebastian and even seems to fall in love with him although they do not appear to be lovers in the novel. Charles, while recounting his lonely and serious childhood, credits Sebastian with giving him a second, happier childhood through their joint escapades, even though those escapades include drinking heavily and spending lavish amounts of money on clothes and cigars.

The novel chronicles Sebastian's descent into an alcoholic haze, beginning with a drunk driving incident and ending with him very ill, nearly destitute (despite the money his family sends him), and living with monks in Tunis. Through Cordelia's report, the Brideshead family and Charles learn that

Sebastian has become religious.

Hardcastle

A friend of Sebastian's at Oxford, Hardcastle regularly loaned him his convertible, two-seater Morris-Cowley car.

Mrs. Hawkins

Mrs. Hawkins is the childhood nanny to Sebastian, his older brother, and two sisters. She still lives at Brideshead in an out-of-the-way room. Nanny Hawkins is much loved by the four Brideshead children, so much so that Sebastian makes a special trip out to his home to have Charles meet her. She is a devout Catholic.

Mr. Hooper

Mr. Hooper is Charles Ryder's new platoon commander as the novel opens. Charles does not particularly trust Mr. Hooper to accomplish a task but claims to have affection for him because he tolerated being the focus of an embarrassing incident. Charles views Hooper as a symbol of "Young England," with his relaxed dress and attitude.

Jasper

Jasper is Charles's older cousin. He has been at Oxford for a few years and is very fond of giving

Charles advice on how he should live his life and spend his money, what classes to take, what clubs to belong to, how to wear his clothes, and whom to associate with. Charles does not follow any of his suggestions. Jasper visits Charles toward the end of his first year at Oxford and scolds him for hanging out with a "bad set" and getting drunk frequently.

Kurt

Kurt is a young German who lives with Sebastian in Algeria and then follows him to Greece. He left Germany to join the French Foreign Legion but ended up in Fez, sick and apparently living off Sebastian. There is some indication that they may be lovers.

Lunt

Lunt is Charles's valet at Oxford, also referred to as his "scout." He is very patient with Charles concerning his carousing and drinking.

Father MacKay

Father MacKay is the priest brought in by Brideshead to give Lord Marchmain his last rites. Lord Marchmain sends him away, very politely, the first time he shows up. Father MacKay is very eager to give Lord Marchmain his last rites, so he makes a second, successful attempt when Lord Marchmain is semi-conscious.

Lord Alex Marchmain

Lord Marchmain is Sebastian's father. He left the family at the time of World War I, when he went to Italy, and never returned. He lives in Venice with his mistress, Cara.

He and Lady Marchmain have never divorced because of her strong Catholic beliefs, of which he is openly disdainful. Lord Marchmain will agree to nearly anything his children ask of him if he thinks it will upset Lady Marchmain. Cara believes that he truly hates his wife.

Lord Marchmain returns to Brideshead after Lady Marchmain's death when he knows that he himself is near death. His death and his apparent acceptance of last rites have a profound effect on Charles and Julia's feelings about Catholicism and religion.

Lady Teresa Marchmain

Lady Marchmain is Sebastian's mother. She is separated from Lord Marchmain and has a companion, the poet Sir Adrian Porson. She is devoutly Roman Catholic and even has tried to convert Charles. She is very fond of Charles and tries to recruit him to help Sebastian stop drinking. She dies just before World War II.

Marquis of Marchmain

See Lord Alex Marchmain

Marquise of Marchmain

See Lady Teresa Marchmain

Julia Mottram

See Lady Julia Flyte

Rex Mottram

Rex is Lady Julia's boyfriend and eventually her fiancé and husband. He is originally from Canada, which prompts many to see him as an inferior match for Julia. He is presented as somewhat stupid and dull when he takes lessons in Catholicism before marrying Julia. He is handsome and seems very open with information about himself and his business dealings. Ironically, his past catches up with him when he tries to marry Julia in the Catholic Church, and Brideshead discovers that he has been married before.

Rex is a member of Parliament and a businessman who knows all the right people and is always offering to connect friends and colleagues with one another. He bails out Charles, Sebastian, and Boy Mulcaster when they are thrown in jail and suggests a physician he knows for Lady Marchmain and a place where Sebastian can get treatment for alcoholism.

Eventually, Julia separates from Rex, and after

two years she secures a divorce. His political power increases during World War II.

Boy Mulcaster

Boy Mulcaster is Sebastian and Anthony's friend who seems to always be in trouble. Charles does not like him although he becomes his brother-in-law when Charles marries Celia, Boy's sister.

Celia Mulcaster

Celia is Boy Mulcaster's sister and, eventually, Charles' wife. She has two children with Charles before they agree to a separation and eventual divorce.

Celia is charming, loves to give parties, and easily makes friends. She is unfaithful to Charles just before he leaves for Mexico and Central America for a two-year working trip. They separate when Charles returns, and he falls in love with Julia; they eventually divorce. Celia then marries Robin, a man who is seven years her junior.

Viscount Mulcaster

See Boy Mulcaster

Beryl Muspratt

Beryl Muspratt is Brideshead's fiancée and eventually his wife toward the end of the novel. She is the widow of Admiral Muspratt, a collector of matchboxes, and has three children. Beryl is a devout Catholic, and Brideshead is worried that she will be offended if she is asked to come to Brideshead Castle while Julia and Charles are there, living together outside of marriage.

Father Phipps

Father Phipps is a priest brought to Brideshead to conduct mass. He appears to be somewhat a fool because he believes that Sebastian and Charles are interested in cricket even when they keep telling him that they know nothing about the sport.

Charles Ryder

Charles Ryder is the novel's narrator: everything the reader sees and knows is told through his eyes. He first appears as a captain in the English army during World War II, stationed in the Scottish countryside. He is a man who is filled with memories, a bit nostalgic for an earlier time in his life.

Later in the novel, Charles is in his first year at Oxford, studying history. He is very eager to do the right things in this new environment. When he meets Sebastian, he is swept off his feet by his charm and immediately becomes deeply and exclusively involved with his new friend. He feels that, as child who had a grim, rather serious childhood, he is finally being given a chance to have fun. He and Sebastian spend time together drinking, attending parties, and avoiding their studies.

Charles is a budding artist and painter and occasionally works on a mural at Brideshead Castle, Sebastian's home. Eventually he leaves Oxford, sensing that he is not accomplishing much, and attends art school in Paris. He becomes a relatively well-known painter of buildings and architectural subjects.

Charles at one point declares himself an agnostic, but he is curious about what it means to be a Catholic. Lady Marchmain has many talks with him in her attempt to convert him to Roman Catholicism, but Charles steadfastly believes religion to be useless. At the end of the novel, at Lord Marchmain's death, he seems to have a sort of religious epiphany when he kneels and prays for the dying man.

His marriage to Celia ends in divorce when he meets Julia, after not seeing her for a number of years, and falls in love with her.

Edward Ryder

Edward Ryder is Charles's father, who lives with his household staff in London. He is in his late fifties, but Charles says that he could be mistaken for a man in his seventies or even eighties.

Edward and Charles have a distant relationship. Charles seems to rely on his father for money and not much else. He mentions that his father gave him no advice on being at Oxford. Edward has an odd sense of humor, and people around him often find it difficult to know if he is making an obscure joke or simply behaving strangely.

Mr. Sammy Samgrass

Mr. Samgrass is an Oxford don originally hired by Lady Marchmain to pull together a memoir of her three dead brothers. He is asked to keep an eye on Sebastian when he returns to school for his second year. He appears to be a man who wants only to help the family set their drunken son straight but is ultimately revealed to have taken advantage of their generosity and faith in him. On a foreign trip with Sebastian he is asked to keep track of Sebastian but loses him and tries to hide this fact from Lady Marchmain.

Religion and Catholicism

Brideshead Revisited is filled with references to its characters' views on religion. Charles Ryder is an agnostic, having received little or no religious training as a child, and each member of the Flyte family presents a different image of a Catholic. Charles' cousin Jasper advises him in book one, chapter one, "Beware of the Anglo-Catholics— they're all sodomites with unpleasant accents. In fact, steer clear of all the religious groups; they do nothing but harm." Throughout the novel, Charles questions members of the Flyte family about their beliefs and even makes light of religion until his epiphany at the end of the book.

Sebastian is a believer but has trouble staying within the rules and strictures of Catholicism. "Oh dear, it's very difficult being a Catholic," he notes in book one, chapter four. In that same chapter, he and Charles have their first discussion, of many, about Catholicism, and Charles expresses great amazement that Sebastian believes the "awful lot of nonsense" that Catholics ascribe to, such as the story of Christ's birth. "Is it nonsense? I wish it were. It sometimes sounds terribly sensible to me," answers Sebastian. His life is a struggle between what he wants to do and what he believes his church requires him to do. After years of drunkenness and wandering around the world, Sebastian ends up as an aide at a monastery in Tunis, in a sense returning to his religion while still being very much a worldly man.

Lord Marchmain is openly disdainful of Catholicism, having rejected the Church when he left Lady Marchmain. Like Sebastian, he appears to come back to his religion in book two, chapter five when, on his deathbed, he mutely signals that he is sorry for his sins in response to a priest's questions. Charles's response upon witnessing this, despite his previous dismissal of religion and Catholicism, is to say a brief prayer under his breath. Lady Marchmain is adamantly Catholic and in book one, chapter five announces that the Flyte family "must make a Catholic of Charles." The fact that she will not give Lord Marchmain a divorce is attributed to her being a devout Catholic.

When Cordelia is young, she attends a convent, and she tells Charles that because he is an agnostic she will pray for him. Her love of religion at that age takes typically childlike forms, such as saying a novena (a series of prayers recited for nine days) for a dead pet, but as an adult, her love of God is manifested in pursuing good works as a nurse during wartime. She is the only Catholic character who truly seems to enjoy her religion and her relationship with God. Brideshead is a Catholic strictly because he was born one—he has no real interest in or passion for the subject. Most of his utterances about religion are legalistic, such as when he discovers that Rex cannot marry Julia in the Catholic Church because he is divorced.

Julia appears throughout most of the book to be uninterested in her Catholicism, except as it is a barrier to marrying her social equal. Only toward the end of the novel, after she has started her affair with Charles and divorces Rex, does she begin to think about being a Catholic. Even though she loves Charles, she expresses concern that her behavior—her "waywardness and wilfulness, a less disciplined habit than most of her contemporaries" when she was a young girl, as well as her illicit affair with Charles—has filled her with sin. When she tells Charles after her father's death that she can no longer see him, she admits, "I've always been bad. Probably I shall be bad again, punished again. But the worse I am, the more I need God." The Epilogue finds Charles saying a small prayer in the chapel at Brideshead, and he is pleased that the chapel is open years after he has last seen the family.

Alcoholism

The novel provides an overview of how Sebastian's family and friends react to his increasingly destructive reliance on alcohol. At first, Sebastian seems to be a typical college student, drinking frequently, but always with friends and never suffering an unhappy consequence. Charles notices that the amount of Sebastian's drinking, as well as his generally happy demeanor, changes when they return to Oxford after their blissful summer at Brideshead mansion.

A number of incidents follow that mark the beginning of the end of the close friendship between Charles and Sebastian. After a party in London, Sebastian drives drunk with other people in the car, including Charles, and is stopped by the police. They are all taken to jail. During Easter at Brideshead, Sebastian is drinking heavily, missing meals, and treating Charles badly. He accuses Charles of spying on him for the family and eventually leaves for London.

Topics For Further Study

- Research the Spanish Civil War and how the numerous volunteers from all over the world played a part. Where did they come from, and why did they volunteer for what was often dangerous duty?

- How does Charles's college life compare to your school experiences?

Write an essay in which you consider the similarities and differences.

- Think about how Sebastian's drinking is described and dealt with in the novel. Are attitudes about drinking different today? How do the Flytes handle Sebastian's drinking problem, and how does this compare to the way similar problems are handled today?

- If possible, find someone who lived through the Great Depression in the United States or elsewhere. Interview the person to learn what life was like then, and how it was different from life today. If you are unable to interview someone, read first-hand accounts of depression-era people and write an essay describing their way of life during that period.

- When Sebastian wants to escape his family, he travels to the Middle East and North Africa. When Charles Ryder leaves his wife to paint and draw for two years, he goes to Mexico and Central America. Why do you think each chose the place he did? Where would you go to if you wanted to get away for a while?

- Think about the transatlantic cruise Charles and Celia take from New

York to London. Imagine what it would be like to travel with a group of strangers on a ship that takes days to get to Europe. Write a series of diary entries as if you were Charles or Celia describing the trip and your feelings and experiences. You may want to do some historical research to help you make your entries accurate and detailed.

The family's response to Sebastian's drinking is a classic case of denial. At Easter, no one in the family is willing to face what is happening to Sebastian, instead seeking out Charles to fix it for them. Lady Marchmain asks Charles about Sebastian's behavior. Charles covers for his friend, say-ing that Sebastian is getting a cold. Julia acknowledges to Charles that she knows of her brother's drinking but tells Charles that he must take care of Sebastian. "Well, you must deal with him. It's no business of mine," she says. Brideshead also asks Charles to help Sebastian stop drinking, and Lady Marchmain expects Charles to keep an eye on Sebastian. "You've got to help him. I can't," she pleads.

Eventually, a dean finds Sebastian wandering around the university drunk. The school agrees to allow him to stay if he moves in with a monsignor (a member of the Roman Catholic clergy), something that Sebastian absolutely refuses to do.

Sebastian leaves Oxford and sets out on a trip to the Middle East with Mr. Samgrass as his guardian, as arranged by his mother. This trip, rather than helping Sebastian, launches him on a lifetime of drinking and wandering around the Middle East and North Africa. Charles and Sebastian see each other only briefly after Sebastian leaves Oxford.

Male Friendship

Sebastian and Charles's friendship is an intense one. In fact, while their relationship appears to be platonic, the words Charles uses to describe their relationship border on the romantic. The picnic they take together in book one, chapter one is portrayed in dreamy and romantic terms:

> We lay on our backs, Sebastian's eyes on the leaves above him, mine on his profile … and the sweet scent of the tobacco merged with the sweet summer scents around us and the fumes of the sweet, golden wine seemed to lift us a finger's breadth above the turf and hold us suspended.

Cara, Lord Marchmain's mistress, notes the closeness between the two friends and surprises Charles by asking him about it in book one, chapter four. She approves of relationships between young men, "if they do not go on too long," and adds that at their young age it is better "to have that kind of love for another boy than for a girl."

The intensity of Charles and Sebastian's friendship transforms Charles. He changes his group of friends at Oxford after meeting Sebastian, and he even alters how his room is decorated and the books he reads based on what Sebastian and his friends like. Charles also becomes deeply involved with Sebastian's family, and they come to think of him almost as one of their own. When Charles is later involved in his love affair with Julia, Sebastian's sister, he indicates that Sebastian was the "forerunner," the first person in the Flyte family with whom he fell in love. This all-encompassing friendship makes Sebastian's eventual drunkenness and depression especially painful for Charles.

Memories and Reminiscences

The entire novel is drawn as a series of Charles's memories; indeed, the novel's subtitle, *The Sacred and Profane Memories of Captain Charles Ryder*, makes this clear. The book opens in the present with Charles surprised to discover that he is encamped near Brideshead mansion, which sets off the memories that make up the body of the book. The novel closes with him in the present again and briefly walking through the house, running into Nanny Hawkins and savoring a few more memories about his friendship with the Flyte family.

As well, Charles is a man who values the past, whether imagined or real. Book one is entitled "Et In Arcadia Ego," which is Latin for "I, too, lived in Arcadia," referring to a pastoral and mountainous region of ancient Greece used extensively in painting and literature to denote a sort of Utopia, or a place where life is wonderful and well lived. Book one tells the story of meeting Sebastian, and the blissful time they spent together.

Throughout the novel, Charles believes that what *was* is preferable to what *is;* in the Prologue he complains about the current behavior of "Young England." He bemoans young people's lack of an education, their dress, and their manner of speech. Even as a student at Oxford, he complains, as book one opens, when women arrive for a week of dances and parties. The change in atmosphere at his school upsets him.

All of Charles' memories of Sebastian during their first year as friends are romanticized. In book one, chapter four, for example, Charles fondly remembers a summer, spent almost always alone with Sebastian, when, "I, at any rate, believed myself to be very near heaven, during those languid days at Brideshead." And Sebastian, as well, realizes that this summer of their youth will be something they always look back on: "If it could only be like this always—always summer, always alone, the fruit always ripe."

Style

Point of View

Brideshead Revisited is written completely from the first person point-of-view; that is, solely through the eyes of Charles Ryder. Charles is the only one telling the story, so the reader must decide whether he is a reliable or an unreliable narrator. Are his impressions of the events and characters in the story to be believed?

In general, Charles is a trustworthy narrator. He does not obviously exaggerate or provide unbelievable information. But, when only one person is telling a story, that person's background and experiences color the telling of the tale. In Charles' case, his childhood was a serious one, with very little happiness. His mother died when he was young and his father pays little attention to him. The absence of his own family may have made it easy for him to become intimately involved with the Flyte family, and because of this closeness he may be blind to some of their faults. A number of times other characters refer to the less-than-wonderful characteristics of the Flytes, including Sebastian, and this either confuses or upsets Charles.

Charles tells the story of his relationship with the Flytes and Sebastian with the benefit of hindsight. He has had time during the intervening fifteen to twenty years to reconsider events. The story is framed by the present, with a Prologue and an Epilogue, but takes place primarily in the past.

Satire

Waugh is well-known for his satirical novels, books that make fun of social customs and the people who participate in them. While *Brideshead Revisited* is not truly a satirical work and marks a change in Waugh's writing style, he does not completely abandon this favored technique. Satire is found in the book, particularly where religion is concerned. Depictions of priests are not always complementary. For example, the priest who visits Brideshead during Charles and Sebastian's summer vacation can't seem to understand that the two friends know nothing about cricket, even though they tell him this repeatedly. In addition to making subtle fun of Rex Mottram and his eagerness to be an important political player, Rex is made to look dim-witted when he takes classes to convert to Catholicism. And when issues of Catholic doctrine are discussed, such as how the final rites should be given to Lord Marchmain, everyone in the Flyte family seems to have a different and confused impression as to the correct way.

Romance

Romantic settings and events are prevalent in *Brideshead Revisited*. Romantic technique in a work of fiction refers to the use of language that is flowery or characters and events that are idealized.

Waugh employs what critic James F. Carens calls "purple" language and draws almost fantasy images of a number of characters.

Charles's two most serious relationships, with Sebastian and his sister Julia, are pursued in the countryside, in idealized pastoral settings. Charles and Sebastian have a picnic early in their relationship, and at Brideshead they spend a summer that is described as "near heaven." He and Julia move to Brideshead to continue their love affair in the country. In book two, chapter three, for example, one evening at Brideshead is remembered as "tranquil, lime-scented," and Julia is pictured "in a tight little gold tunic and a white gown, one hand in the water idly turning an emerald ring to catch the fire of the sunset." Waugh's language here is almost dreamlike.

Setting in Time

The novel's main action takes place in England between World War I and World War II. While international events barely impact the story line, Waugh drops numerous hints in the narrative to help the reader know what is happening outside of the characters' immediate surroundings.

The Prologue and the Epilogue take place in a wartime encampment in the English countryside. When women are part of an event at Oxford early in the novel, Charles's servant comments that such a thing would not have happened before World War I. Numerous hints are given that war with Germany and Italy is on the horizon. When Rex returns to Brideshead with his political friends, the conversation is filled with references to running into fake tanks in the Black Forest and to leaders such as Franco and Chamberlain. One of the reasons Lord Marchmain gives for moving back to England is the "international situation."

Simile

Augmenting the relatively rich language in *Brideshead Revisited*, Waugh occasionally uses similes. These are phrases that compare two seemingly unlike things. For example, in book one, chapter five, Charles compares Sebastian to "a Polynesian," happy when left alone but threatened when "the big ship dropped anchor beyond the coral reef." In book two, chapter one, Charles remarks that bats in a cave "hung in the dome like dry seed-pods." These images contribute to the nostalgic and lush tone of the novel's language.

Historical Context

The Pre-War Years and World War II

The book's events take place between 1922 and World War II. Charles Ryder's generation at Oxford was one that found itself too young to fight in the first war but well into its thirties by the time the Second World War erupted. Throughout the body of *Brideshead Revisited*, Waugh indicates that something is brewing outside the walls of the stately mansions and colleges where most of the novel's actions take place. Europe between World War I and World War II was a place of both great prosperity and dismal poverty, of social innovations and political disarray.

As an adult, Cordelia serves as a nurse during the Spanish Civil War, which lasted from 1936 to 1939. This war was fought between the Nationalists, who were fascists supported by the Italian and German governments, and the Loyalists, who were supported by many thousands of volunteers from other nations. When it was all over, hundreds of thousands were dead, and a fascist regime held power in Spain. The Nazis in Germany took note that other European governments were reluctant to step into the fray; this isolationism indicated that Europe might not interfere in the Nazis' own plans for world domination.

Germany suffered great losses during the First World War and was in political and economic disarray after the war. By the early 1930s, Germany's military and economic might began to recover under Adolf Hitler. By the middle of the 1930s, Hitler's political party, the Nazi Party, was firmly in command. Germany began to make territorial claims on other parts of Europe in the late 1930s. European leaders, including those of England, desperately wanted to avoid another world war, so they capitulated to Germany's demands. British Prime Minister Neville Chamberlain signed the Munich Pact, hoping that Germany would hold to its promise that the Sudetenland, a part of Czechoslovakia, would be its last aggressive territorial claim. The effort at appeasing the Nazi government did not work, and Germany continued to invade other countries. In September 1939, Germany invaded Poland, and Great Britain and France jointly declared war on Germany. The war spread to nearly every corner of the globe, including Africa and Asia, and ultimately involved the United States, Russia, Japan, Italy, and others. By the time the war ended in 1945, a year after Waugh finished writing *Brideshead Revisited*, the United Kingdom alone had sustained more than nine hundred thousand military and civilian casualties.

Economic Depression

After World War I, England suffered serious economic decline, yet the privileged classes continued to consume at a fever pitch. The Flytes are a fabulously wealthy family, although by the late 1920s Rex reports that the family is having some money difficulties.

England's coal, steel, cotton, and shipping industries were in serious financial trouble by the mid-1920s. Coal miners initiated incidences of labor unrest and struck for improvements in their working situations in 1925. The following year, England's General Strike involved some six million union workers. This event prompts Charles and several fellow English art students to leave Paris for their homeland, to see how they can be of help. However, the strike lasted only six days. The economic bad news continued, however, and 1929 brought a stock market crash. The crash and the resulting Great Depression had global effects, and the misery spawned by the worldwide economic downturn contributed to the rise of the Nazi Party in Germany.

Literature

English and American literature from World War I to 1944, when Waugh finished writing *Brideshead Revisited*, was very diverse. Authors experimented with a variety of forms and styles and dealt with subjects formerly considered risqué, such as sex; D. H. Lawrence's novel *Lady Chatterley's Lover* is one example. The horrors of the First World War and the Great Depression prompted writers to consider a world where the old rules had failed, and many traditional religious, political, and social institutions no longer held the authority they once did. Ernest Hemingway and John Steinbeck were two American writers who captured these feelings of disillusionment, and in 1932 British author Aldous Huxley published his futuristic novel, *Brave New World*, in which he expresses a deep-seated suspicion of totalitarian government and societal uniformity.

In *Brideshead Revisited*, Anthony Blanche, as a student at Oxford, recites a passage from T. S. Eliot's poem *The Waste Land*. This work, published in 1922, focused on loss of faith and on the destruction of civilization as previously understood. It was a huge hit with the post-World War I generation that had witnessed how far human nature could degenerate. The poem questions the premise that civilization is progressing. So ingrained did this work become in that generation's consciousness that college students everywhere, like Anthony Blanche, memorized its lines.

Critical Overview

The reviews of *Brideshead Revisited* ranged from adoring to condemning when the book was first published in 1945. James F. Carens in *The Satiric Art of Evelyn Waugh* notes that while the magazine *Catholic World* raved about the novel and called it "a work of art," critic Edmund Wilson (as quoted by Carens) was less positive. Even though Wilson was an admirer of Waugh's earlier, more satirical works, he called *Brideshead Revisited* "disastrous" and declared that the author "no longer knows his way." John K. Hutchens, reviewing the novel in 1945 for the *New York Times*, wrote that the novel "has the depth and weight that are found in a writer working in his prime."

Carens encourages readers to weigh the book carefully, advising, "A novel that has provoked such diverse views deserves consideration. It may be an imperfect work; it can scarcely be a vapid one." Indeed, despite many critics' disappointment with the book's lack of satirical sharpness, *Brideshead Revisited* is the book that introduced American audiences to Waugh.

Compare & Contrast

- **1920s and 1930s:** The African-American singer and dancer Josephine Baker creates a sensation in Paris with her risqué nightclub show in which she wears an outfit made primarily of feathers. When Anthony and Charles go to a jazz club in London, Charles alludes to having gone to such clubs in Paris, where this kind of entertainment is more accepted than it is in London.

Today: African American Queen Latifah is one of the most prominent performers in the world. She has starred in a television series, hosted her own talk show, been featured in television commercials, and produced top-selling albums.

- **1920s and 1930s:** Art Deco is the primary artistic style. The name is derived from a 1925 exhibition of decorative and industrial arts in Paris. Art Deco style incorporates straight lines and symmetry using manufactured rather than naturally occurring materials. Charles's art is not influenced by this modern style; he prefers more traditional subjects and styles.

  Today: Art Deco is considered a "retro" style but is still widely appreciated and collected. Web sites devoted to preserving and studying Art Deco buildings and decorative objects number in the hundreds and are based around the world, from

New Zealand to Washington, D.C., to Miami.

- **1920s and 1930s:** The period between World War I and World War II is marked by both prosperity and economic crisis worldwide. European nations are working to rebuild after the First World War. After the stock market crash of 1929, much of the industrialized world suffers through record high unemployment and inflation. Wealthy families like the Flytes are somewhat insulated from the devastation by their inherited land and capital.

  Today: Most of the industrialized world has enjoyed at least four years of unparalleled economic prosperity. Among the wealthiest individuals in the world are those who started innovative companies in the high-technology industry, which is fueling economies worldwide.

Much of the negative criticism of *Brideshead Revisited* has charged that in this book, Waugh leaves his earlier empire of hard-bitten satire and wades into the gentler world of romance. Some critics, such as Paul Fussell in the *New Republic*, appear to suggest that Waugh has become soft in his middle age. Comparing *Brideshead Revisited* with

Waugh's short stories written in the 1930s, Fussell argues:

> If in that overripe fantasy, manufactured in the grim 1940s, he seems at pains to register his worshipful intimacy with the aristocracy, in these stories of the 1930s he exhibits for the unearned-income set an intellectual and moral disdain hard to distinguish from that of a contemporary Marxist-Leninist. If he'd conceived Sebastian Flyte in 1935, he'd have little trouble discerning from the start the selfishness, cruelty, and fatuity behind those expensive good looks.

For many critics, *Brideshead Revisited* marks a change in Waugh's style that continues for the rest of his writing life. Richard P. Lynch, in *Papers on Language and Literature*, remarks that Waugh's later novels, except for *The Loved One*, "are more reassuring to readers of conventional romance." The fact that the novel is completely created from the mist of Charles Ryder's memories gives it a certain wistful quality that his earlier novels lack. In fact, Lynch says in his criticism that it is "atypical among Waugh's novels in its triumph of sentiment over satire."

But others argue that *Brideshead Revisited* still has some of the satire and sharpness of the earlier novels, but it is done in a more mature and learned way. Hutchens argues in his *New York Times* review that the story of Charles and the Flyte family contains much of the "deadly use of detail, the scorn of vulgarity, the light summary touch with minor characters," such as Anthony Blanche and Charles's father. But in this new novel there is now "one sentence and one paragraph after another of reflection and description, [which] could have found no place in the staccato atmosphere of his other works." In Hutchens's eyes, *Brideshead Revisited* is a more fully-grown novel, benefiting from the narrator's years of distance from the story's events and characters and from the author's own maturity.

This assertion of maturity does not sit well, though, with some critics. Barry Ulanov, in *The Vision Obscured: Perceptions of Some Twentieth-Century Catholic Novelists*, cites *Brideshead Revisited* as evidence of Waugh's midcareer decline. Echoing Lynch, Ulanov argues that most of Waugh's books after 1945 "are blighted by the disease of Brideshead, an egregious inclination to take religion seriously, accompanied by a marked distaste for the world that does not share that inclination—the modern world."

In fact, Waugh's own worldview can be seen in such novels as *Brideshead Revisited*, in which there is a sense that the past is preferable to the present and that the current generation has lost touch with the values and graciousness of its history. According to Ulanov, Waugh, in his own life, "became a furious partisan, fighting for the survival of ancient values, ancient worlds, ancient rituals." As a Catholic, he worked against the reforms of the Second Vatican Council, which promoted such changes as translating the Latin of the Mass into English.

Waugh's Catholicism and how it is reflected and used in his novels is a continuing subject for critics. Most agree that the author's conservative and traditional outlook is revealed in his work, but while Carens notes that *Brideshead Revisited* is the first of Waugh's books where his interest in Roman Catholicism is so broadly exhibited, he declares that the novel is not an apology for Catholicism. "It is not a preachy book," he asserts. As Carens points out, readers can see evidence of Waugh's past satiric craftsmanship; satire is blended with religion in the book, specifically where the confused Flyte family is discussing whether the dying Lord Marchmain should receive last rites from a priest. "Over this entire scene Waugh has cast his satirical irony; the scene exists for novelistic purposes rather than dogmatic reasons," writes Carens. And the difficulty of Catholicism in Britain, as portrayed in the novel, might well erase any critic's concerns that the book slips into romance, according to Frank Kermode in *Encounter*. To the Flytes, their religion is a burden to shoulder, for "only in misery, it seems, will the Faith be restored in the great families of England."

Whether *Brideshead Revisited* is a book without any teeth or evidence of a writer's development is a topic that critics will continue to debate. But the novel has withstood the test of time, as it was recently cited by the editorial board of the Modern Library as one of the 100 best English language books of the twentieth century.

Sources

Burdett, Paul S., Jr., "Author Evelyn Waugh Served Honorably in the British Army as an SAS Commando," in *World War II*, Vol. 14, No. 1, May 1999, p. 16.

Carens, James F., *The Satiric Art of Evelyn Waugh*, University of Washington Press, 1966, pp. 98-110.

Fussell, Paul, "The Genesis of a Snob," in *New Republic*, Vol. 187, No. 3542, December 6, 1982, pp. 38-39.

Hutchens, John K., "Evelyn Waugh's Finest Novel," in *New York Times*, December 30, 1945.

Kermode, Frank, "Mr. Waugh's Cities," in *Encounter*, Vol. 15, No. 5, November, 1960, pp. 63-66, 68-70.

Lynch, Richard P., "Evelyn Waugh's Early Novels: the Limits of Fiction," in *Papers on Language and Literature*, Vol. 30, No. 4, Fall 1994, pp. 373-86.

Ulanov, Barry, "The Ordeal of Evelyn Waugh," in *The Vision Obscured: Perceptions of Some Twentieth-Century Catholic Novelists*, edited by Melvin J. Friedman, Fordham University Press, 1970, pp. 79-93.

Further Reading

Allitt, Patrick, *Catholic Converts*, Cornell University Press, 2000.

> Waugh is among a significant group of British and American intellectuals who, during the nineteenth and the early twentieth centuries, converted to Catholicism. This recently published book is an account of the impact these converts had on the Catholic Church.

Cannadine, David, *The Decline and Fall of the British Aristocracy*, Vintage Books, 1999.

> This book tracks the British aristocracy from its supremacy in the 1870s to the 1930s, when it had lost a generation of sons to World War I and much of its wealth as well.

Stannard, Martin, ed., *Evelyn Waugh*, Routledge, 1997.

> This text is one of the major biographies of Waugh, covering his life from the 1920s through to his death.

Wykes, David, *Evelyn Waugh: A Literary Life*, St. Martin's Press, 1999.

> Wykes's book explores how Waugh's

life affected his writing, but this is more a work of literary criticism than a biography.